petals
OF PURPOSE

Petals
of Purpose

Crafting a Life of Meaning Through Plants

Cindy Hernandez

ALEgRÍA
PUBLISHING

Introduction

In the whirlwind of motherhood and the challenges of living with endometriosis, I often found myself overwhelmed by the weight of my emotions. My journey through depression felt isolating until I discovered a surprising ally: plants. This book chronicles my transformation through nurturing a small collection of greenery, each leaf and blossom becoming a source of solace and strength.

As I learned to care for my plants, I developed vital coping skills that helped me navigate my mental health struggles. In these pages, you will find not only my personal story but also a practical guide to starting your own plant collection. With interactive journaling prompts, you will explore your feelings, reflect on your journey, and cultivate both your plants and your well-being. Join me in discovering how the simple act of nurturing life can inspire healing, resilience, and joy amidst the chaos.

Forward by Gabriella Cervantes

Cindy opens her inner world as she shares firsthand experiences with depression and how the very plants she was tending reciprocated that same love she gave them. Her journey shows the day-to-day choices she makes to heal not only herself, but other plant enthusiasts that need love and care. Cindy goes from self-isolation as a coping mechanism to being surrounded by a community who embraced her charm and love for her green friends.

- Gabriella Cervantes

Chapter by Chapter

*Just like plants, we need the right amount
of light to grow and shine brightly.*

Chapter 1
Boxes and Borders:
A Journey to Self-Discovery

I was raised to be a wife and mother. The only daughter and youngest of three siblings, there were a lot of expectations placed on me. My immigrant, El Salvadoran, single mother had us moving every six to nine months, fleeing the father I never met. Despite not being able to feel grounded, I found stability in becoming a good Latina woman. I also found moving and meeting new people and discovering new places throughout Los Angeles County, California to be an adventure. I learned to keep my items in boxes because eventually I would get the news that it was time to go. Eventually, it was no longer an adventure. By the time I was twelve, I started to realize it was a lonely, unstable life; I didn't have any genuine friendships or positive memories to look back on. One of the reasons I didn't like making friends is because I knew I would lose touch when there was no Facebook, Instagram, or any type of digital media to keep track of people in the early '90s... Being the child of a single mother, resources that are available today were luxuries I couldn't ask for. It would hurt too much when people disappeared from my life. So, like my belongings and feelings, people went into boxes when I left on the next leg of my journey.

Growing up I never really understood my culture. My mother wanted my brother and I to be highly educated, American children. She didn't allow us to watch TV or listen to music in Spanish because she didn't want us to have an accent when we spoke English. She spoke to us in Spanish, and we would respond to her in English. I remember people being taken aback by our communication style while out in public.

Growing up I had trouble fitting in with other Latino children because I was not exposed to my Mexican culture. I remember the looks of confusion and disgust when I would confess that I'm not a fan of beans, Pozole, or Menudo. I didn't understand the problem and would feel embarrassed if I was invited to a party and didn't want to try the food. Others saw me as disrespectful and a picky eater. When pressed, I would eat just to fit in. I also remember the rejection I felt when confessing I don't like banda music. I was a "no sabo kid" before it was a thing. If you could see the look on my friends' faces on the playground when I told them I had no idea who Rosa Salvaje was, and I had never seen a novela. The only thing that would save me in my group of friends was my love for Mana and Heroes del Silencio–aka Rock en español. Although I wasn't able to speak the Spanish language until I was fifteen, I understood every single melody. It's how I learned the language.

At home I felt pressure for perfection. I had to cook, bake, and clean, and I had to do everything right the first time. I had very little time to play because I had to learn to place the bacon in the right place on the plate for my future husband. As a child, I thought it would be fun to be like Harriet from Ozzie & Harriet or Lucy from I Love Lucy. When I was able to enjoy free time, I spent it with my dolls. I would give them a bath, dress them, and comb their hair. I would prepare them food with my tea set and pretend to do their laundry. I would get them ready for school and prepare a snack for when they got home. My mother would jokingly praise me for being such a good mom. My fondest memories were of preparing my dolls for bed, tucking them in, and saying prayers with them, which frustrated my mom because of how long it took me to put myself to bed. Growing up in the lifestyle we were living, I needed to be grateful for what I received since toys were only given on Christmas and birthdays. I looked forward to these holidays because I knew I'd be adding a new member to my family, I'd be getting a new doll. Even though life was unstable, my dolls gave me stability and love.

At age thirteen, I started to wake up to the reality around me. My dolls no longer gave me joy, and I started to feel the pressure of young adulthood. I worked hard at school even though I could barely read and was horrible at math. I was made fun of and bullied for counting on my fingers and stumbling on my words when reading out loud.

As soon as I'd wake up in the morning, I would start my day cleaning. When I returned home from school, I would do even more chores because the work of a mother is never done. En chinga estaba todos los dias sin tener amistades porque las esposa se queda a cuidar su casa.

At fourteen, I started to discover my voice. I asked my Mom, "¿Por qué otra vez nos tenemos que mover si no nos han encontrado?" I can still remember the face I made when my teacher called me out of class to tell me it was my last day at Nimitz Junior High, and I would not be graduating from eighth grade with my friends. It was even more disappointing to know that Bellflower Middle School, where I was transferring, didn't have graduations.

It was in Bellflower that I realized that I did not want an unstable life for my future children. If I was going to be the perfect mom one day, it would not be by making them slaves to perfection and tradition. I would go to bed thinking, I will not do this to my daughter. The cycle had to break. I did not want to teach my future daughter que la vida no es mía, es el niño y por todo es ellos.

At fifteen, instead of a quinceañera, I asked my mother to give me the gift of stability. I requested to finish high school all at the same place and have some positive memories. She saw how important this was to me and did her best to comply. Even though we moved four more times, we stayed in the same city for four years.

"To plant a garden is to believe in tomorrow."
Audrey Hepburn

Chapter 2
Threads of Change:
Crafting a New Future

High school brought a new sense of self. I felt like now was the time to start working on what I wanted my future to be when it came to my career. My mom wanted me to be a teacher, however I had extreme social anxiety and thought I would never be able to speak in public or have patience for children. I would have loved to be a doctor but I have dyslexia, and I had an extreme fear of writing the wrong prescription for someone. So, I didn't think it was possible. I was developing a passion for caring for the environment, but I didn't know how to turn it into a career.. I ended up choosing art.

When you're always moving and poor, you learn to make the best of what you have. I would take old socks and turn them into dresses for my Barbies. I would even make outfits for them out of unconventional materials like napkins, toilet paper, coffee filters and straws. It became a challenge for me. I created belts and hair accessories out of shoelaces, ribbons and rubber bands... This blossomed into a love for fashion. I wanted to pursue fashion and costume design as a career. Crafting became a hobby that helped me pass the time when I grew out of playing with dolls. Now that I had friends I enjoyed making my own greeting cards and creating something unique for gifts.

I met my best friend, Sarah, in history class. She sat in front of me and was on the quiet side. She had blond hair and blue eyes, but I never really paid attention to her since I rarely made friends. She was super smart and always had her work done ahead of schedule. I was usually the last one done, and it was quite embarrassing at times. One day she decided to check on me since her work was done and she was bored and wanted to help me. Word searches and crossword puzzles were the worst for me, but they were her favorite, and she showed me tips and tricks on how to complete them in a timely manner.

Eventually Sarah gave me her phone number and told me to call her. She told me that if we were going to be friends I would need to know everything there is to know about metal music. She started giving playlists and bands to study. This became our bonding time and eventually we would talk about the shows we were watching on tv like The Real World, Daria, and my favorite talk shows. Time with her felt like I finally belonged somewhere. She didn't look down on me for any of my disabilities or where I came from. She simply saw me.

As she got to know me, she introduced me to her friends. They were very smart, kind, and friendly people who liked helping me with my homework. They said it was fun because it was easy, and they eventually started seeing what my problem was. Sarah introduced me to our school guidance counselor who got me help for dyslexia. Once I knew what was going on it was now easier to understand myself however it did make me sad to know that I wasn't like everyone else. Little did I know that this is where I was becoming aware of my depression.

My crafting moments took me away from the barrio y la vecindad we were living in at the time. I could escape the chisme and toxicity my mom would engage in with the nosy neighbor and just have fun. Life in general was so stressful that creativity gave me the chance to escape into a world of my own. I didn't have to worry about fitting in or being perfect or que va decir la gente. I learned a lot of what I was capable of and would push myself to create the visions I saw in my head. Loneliness was no longer there because I wasn't looking for someone else to make me happy. The need for approval or acceptance was also not needed because I was happy with what I created without needing validation from others. It was still difficult to escape my mother who thought my head was always in the clouds instead of focusing on important things. In my moments of creativity, I was creating a secret world that was full of joy; I was free to express myself the way I wished.

I couldn't wait to graduate once I was accepted into a trade school to study fashion. I was looking forward to college instead of dreading having to keep working on academics that were a struggle to keep up with. I could now focus on the direction I wanted to take my life. I wanted to establish my independence and enjoy the college experience. Being away from everyone and everything that caused me to struggle with self-acceptance helped me to figure out who I was.

Once I finished college, I realized that I needed more schooling and experience in order to get a good paying job. My youth made it difficult to find a job in the field I wanted to work in, so I decided to continue my studies and work on a Bachelors of Arts in costume design. In order to do that I needed to take some classes at a community college in order to transfer to a State College or University. At Cerritos Community College, the direction of my life would change forever.

Cindy Hernandez

*The seeds you plant today will
be the garden you enjoy tomorrow.*

Cindy Hernandez

Chapter 3
Canvas of Life: Love, Chaos, and the Pursuit of Happiness

It's funny how a brush stroke can be the beginning of your whole future. On the first day of classes, I was curious about what I was going to learn in my life painting class and a little intimidated by the amount of talent in the room. I'm not a sketch painter, but I wanted to do my best to get the most out of the class. I naturally gravitated to someone I thought was very talented. I didn't find him attractive, but his personality kept me coming back to get advice on how to improve my work. He enjoyed creating just as much as I did, and I was in awe of his natural talent. We both cared about being kind to others and social work, and we liked and listened to the same alternative music as we worked on our painting assignments. One thing that attracted me to him was his carefree spirit. I was always surrounded by rules, authority and perfection, and he was the opposite. He liked to be rebellious and would often do things to catch my attention that would annoy me but make me laugh like smearing my canvas with a paint color I wasn't using. He was so charming and had a way of making me laugh at all the stupidest things. As I sat across the room from him, he would make faces at me, and I would try not to smile.

I still remember the night he proposed. We were studying for finals at Denny's. We were both tired, and out of nowhere he asked if I would marry him. I thought it was a silly question and said yes. He then asked for my hand and put an onion ring on my finger telling me that was my engagement ring. I thought it was a joke, and I said, "Wow, that's a really big ring, but I want a diamond." He started laughing and then asked me for my hand again and ate the onion ring. We finished studying , paid the bill, and asked him to take me home. Once we got to my house he told me to pack my stuff because we were going on a trip. I went to my room, grabbed a duffle bag with some clothes, a camera, and basic items. We did not think that his 1980 Chevy Sprint would make it to Vegas but we both agreed to see how far we could go. There were moments that were scary, but that little car got us there safely.

We had no plan and no idea where to go since it was both our first times there. Once we settled in a hotel, we spent the day walking around and trying to figure out how we were actually going to get married. Google was still very new, we did not think of bringing a laptop with us and phones were not as sophisticated as they are now. So we did the next best thing: we asked a street performer where we needed to go in order to get married. He gave us the direction we needed to go in, and as we were driving around, we saw the wedding chapels available. The one we chose was the Silver Bell Wedding Chapel because the officiant could be a Bon Jovi impersonator. Once we arrived, the judge asked us for our marriage certificate, and we looked at him like a deer in headlights. He explained we needed to go to the registrar recorder's office to be legally married. The office closed at 6:00 PM, and it was already 5:15 PM. We raced down to the office and found out we needed to pay cash, but all we had were cards. We ran to the car and started searching for change like crazy. A man who spoke only Spanish approached us asking for change to catch the bus because his wallet had been stolen. I explained that we also needed cash, and if we weren't able to pay today we wouldn't be able to get married. The man quickly replied with enthusiasm, "Don't worry about it, I will find someone else to help me. Go get married and congratulations."

We made it back to the justice of the peace just in time to complete the process. We then went back to the Silver Bell Chapel only to find out that the Bon Jovi impersonator was not available. We were not going to let that take away our joy, though, and on 07/07/00 at 7:00 PM, we signed the marriage certificate in front of the judge to begin our ceremony. I did not wear a white dress or have a bouquet of flowers. I didn't even walk down the aisle to the traditional wedding song . I wore jeans and a plaid button-down shirt with puffy sleeves! Looking back, I didn't feel worthy of a big, beautiful white wedding. I was also so in love that all those details didn't matter. I wouldn't have done it any other way.

When you're young you think you can do everything and accomplish all of your goals as long as you plan everything out. And I did exactly that. Kids in daycare, working full-time, coming home to prepare dinner and take the kids to their sporting practice. I had everything ready and ran the house exactly the way I was trained when I was a child. It wasn't easy, but everything went fairly smoothly in terms of progress. We had our house, our kids, and decent paying jobs that kept a roof over our heads. We were grateful for what God had given us and leaned on each other for support. Little did I know that the support I needed would not be there when I needed it the most.

It was during my marriage that I discovered my love for plants and rediscovered how much I cared for the environment. Gardening became a hobby to escape from the pressures of being a wife and mother. The problem was that my husband was anti-schedule and anti-rules which made it difficult for me to have our children follow a schedule or rules as well. He was the fun parent that would encourage our children to be rebellious against "Mom's rules," and I was the one that made sure everything was going accordingly. It became frustrating and straining on our once happy marriage full of adventure.

A plant is like a relationship:
With time, attention, and affection it will blossom.

Cindy Hernandez

Chapter 4
Roots of Resilience:
Healing Through Pain and Growth

At twenty-seven, I was feeling the burnout of a stressful marriage, wild children and handling the responsibilities of a full-time job. I wasn't able to pursue my dreams anymore which made me depressed. The responsibilities of running a household were more important, and to top things off, I was having a lot of problems with my reproductive health that my doctor couldn't resolve. I was taking medications to stop an out of control menstrual cycle, and they made me gain one hundred pounds over the next six years. One of my doctors suggested getting my tubes tied to alleviate some of my pain. I looked into a device called Essure which made my problem worse. The Essure device is a permanent birth control implant that was placed in the fallopian tubes to prevent pregnancy. I had persistent pelvic and abdominal pain, abnormal vaginal bleeding, allergy, headaches, fatigue, skin issues, bloating, nausea and depression. I was doing my best to cope, but my anxiety was at an all-time high without being diagnosed. I was in so much pain that I became a slave to my bed unable to do anything productive. Weekends were spent in a hospital getting hydrated, blood transfusions and interferon treatments to replace the blood, iron and nutrients I was losing. By the time I was thirty-six, the doctors found the best solution to be an endometrial ablation procedure that improved my health.

By this time, I didn't know what to do with my life, and I was at an all-time low. Sadly during my illness, I did everything alone. My husband didn't understand the severity of my illness and thought I just had to tough it out. In the early 2000s, endometriosis was still a mystery to doctors and didn't know how to treat the condition. Endometriosis is a disorder in which tissue similar to the tissue that lines the uterus grows outside the uterus in places where it doesn't belong. At the time, the only treatment was a hysterectomy, but I really felt I was too young for that and still wanted to have one more child. When I learned that an ablation could solve my problem. I jumped at the chance to do it but found myself with mixed emotions. The endometrial ablation is a minimally invasive procedure that destroys the lining of the uterus to treat bleeding.

When I woke up from the surgery, I was happy to be alive but heartbroken that I wouldn't be able to bring a third child into the world. I didn't think it would affect me the way it did, and it got to the point where I didn't feel anything anymore. My marriage was very strained at this time seeing my husband have all the fun while I suffered in silence. It felt more like we were roommates. He felt I was being ungrateful for the second chance God gave me in life. What was even more devastating was walking into the kitchen one day to see my husband's unlocked phone on a text message with red heart emojis. At first I thought he was texting his mother, and then I said to myself, "Wait, his mother doesn't text". I grabbed the phone and locked myself in the bathroom. My heart fell into my stomach when I saw that it was another woman that I didn't know that he was texting and saying, "I love you".

To get myself on the path to good health, I started seeing a chiropractor. At this office I would talk to the receptionist a lot about my plants since she had the front desk full of succulents. She recommended I see her uncle who was a Shaman to help me with my back problems and depression. I thought I would take a chance since he was also a plant lover and his practice was plant-based. He taught me about herbalism and how plants are connected to us. It was through him that I learned how to use gardening to work through big emotions, how to trust the Earth to pull me out of my pain,   and how to use my coping skills to become strong again. He also taught me everything I know about propagation and replanting. The only thing he made me promise was that I would never sell what he taught me because this knowledge was a gift that is not to be sold.

"Gardening adds years to your life and life to your years."
Anonymous

Cindy Hernandez

Chapter 5
A Garden of Memories:
Digging deep to find my way

I couldn't fathom why everything seemed to be spiraling out of control. In the chaos, my sanctuary became the worn wooden bench on my front porch, where I'd sink into its weathered embrace at the end of the day, savoring the hues of the sunset and the comforting aroma of freshly brewed coffee. Across the street, my neighbor of two decades stood witness to the highs and lows of my life. Her presence offered solace and stability in all of the turbulence.

Joan, steeped in Jewish tradition, shared tales of her own family upbringing, weaving wisdom and warmth into the fabric of our conversations. Despite her frailty, she exuded a quiet strength that resonated with me. On this particular summer afternoon, as shadows lengthened and burdens weighed heavy, Joan sensed my need for more than mere words.

Silently, she settled beside me, her touch a gentle reassurance. With a delicate gesture, she beckoned me to her home. There amidst the verdant embrace of her collection of cacti and succulents, Joan's generosity knew no bounds. Each plant she entrusted to me carried not just her care, but a glimmer of hope.

In her eyes, I glimpsed an understanding of my pain, a shared journey through life's trials. While I couldn't erase my sorrows, she offered me a respite, a refuge in the quiet beauty of nature. Little did she know, her simple act of kindness would change my life forever.

Despite harboring a modest garden of my own, my collection lacked the vibrant diversity that now graced my home thanks to Joan's gift. Among them stood my lone succulent, an Echeveria that I smuggled from Mexico; its presence a testament to my longing to escape.

Under Joan's patient guidance, my newfound passion flourished. Together we delved into the art of terrariums, each miniature world a canvas for creativity and renewal. With each delicate pruning and careful propagation, I found solace in the rhythm of nature's cycles.

Joan's teachings extended beyond mere gardening techniques; she breathed life into my creativity, urging me to explore the myriad of possibilities of container gardening. As I molded soil and selected vessels, I felt my spirit stir, awakening to the boundless potential within. In the quiet moments spent tending to my growing menagerie, I found not just solace, but a sense of purpose. She left to the spirit world in 2019, but Joan's legacy lived on in every leaf and tendril, a reminder that amidst life's chaos, beauty and joy could still be found, waiting to be nurtured and cherished.

"Nurture your mind with great thoughts,
for you will never go any higher than you think."
Benjamin Disraeli

Chapter 6
Blossoms of Hope:
Finding Beauty in Chaos

During the whirlwind of the pandemic, my life took an unexpected turn. While the world was transforming indoors, cultivating their own verdant havens, my inbox was flooded with inquiries about plant care. Answering countless DMs sparked an idea: why not compile these queries into a comprehensive guide? I may not have been a writer, influencer, or entrepreneur, but my knack for crafting and having an event planning company birthed a lucrative side hustle. Utilizing social media as my platform, I laid the groundwork for my plant shop. As I sifted through the influx of data, I discerned the common needs and desires of budding plant enthusiasts, igniting a new found passion for content creation.

The overwhelming response affirmed my path, injecting a sense of purpose into my days. Managing the deluge of messages not only kept my depressive symptoms at bay but propelled me into a journey of self-discovery. Armed with a bucked list of long neglected aspirations, I embarked on a voyage of self-love, starting with the simplest pleasures and gradually conquering my fears.

Everyone's mental health journey takes its own twists and turns, doesn't it? For me, depression often manifests itself as neglect and isolation. I've always been a bit of a lone wolf, especially when life throws its curve balls my way. When worries pile up like a mountain, my cozy bed becomes my fortress of solitude. But here's the kicker, when you've got a bunch of needy plants relying on you for love and care, you can't just hide under the covers all day. It was a revelation, really. As I formed bonds with my leafy companions, I realized that my world couldn't revolve solely around my bed. Sure it's comfy and safe, but there's a whole jungle out there that needs tending! So, begrudgingly, I peeled myself away from my haven of blankets and began to tend to my green buddies.

And let me tell you, getting my hands dirty in that soil was like a wake-up call for my senses. It grounded me in the present moment while whispering promises of a brighter future. Each moment spent nurturing those little plantitas was an investment in something bigger than myself.

Now, I'll admit, I didn't exactly have a squad of gardening enthusiasts to share my newfound passion with. Apart from Joan, my trusty green-thumb buddy and the knowledgeable shaman, it was mostly a solo gig. But you know what? That was ok. My self-imposed isolation was about shutting out the world; it was about finding my own rhythm, my own routine. And let me tell you, finding that rhythm was key to keeping the momentum going. It was about carving time out of my day for something other than worry and doubt. Because in the end, it's the little things–the daily rituals, the quiet moments of connection– that keep us moving forward one step at a time.

My plant journey mirrored my personal growth, nurturing the confidence I needed to step in front of the camera and engage with my audience unfiltered. Despite my botanical expertise, there were still realms to explore, prompting me to delve into plant hacks and share my findings with eager followers. What began as a solitary pursuit blossomed into a thriving online community, united by a shared passion for greenery. Together, we experimented, exchanged knowledge, and forged connections, bridging the physical distance imposed by the pandemic.

Amidst the chaos of plant care, I recognized the need for a practical tool guide for novices on their journey. Thus, I crafted a workbook brimming with insights and space for personal observations—a roadmap for cultivating green thumbs. The shift from hobbyist to entrepreneur was swift with demand skyrocketing as people sought solace in nurturing living things. What started as a modest hobby of terrariums burgeoned into a bustling enterprise, with orders pouring in by the dozens each week.

Yet, despite the digital camaraderie, there was an undeniable allure to in-person interactions. As restrictions eased, I took my shop on the road, setting up pop-ups, workshops, and attending events to offer firsthand guidance and foster genuine connections.

The first workshop after the pandemic was a long-awaited breath of fresh air. It wasn't just any workshop, it was a gathering born from the desire to learn and grow, both in plant knowledge and community connection. And at its heart was my mentor, a guiding light whose wisdom illuminated the path forward. She, like many of us, understood the power of learning in community. So when the opportunity arose to open up her urban farmhouse in Bell Gardens, CA it felt like fate had intervened. This was our chance not only to delve into the world of plants but to do so surrounded by kindred spirits.

As the event drew near, excitement bubbled within me like a pot about to boil over. I poured my heart and soul into crafting the perfect content, knowing that each world and lesson would be a building block for our shared journey. When I finally shared the news with my followers, the response was nothing short of overwhelming. Joy and anticipation filled the air as nineteen eager souls expressed their interest in attending. Though COVID restrictions limited our numbers to just six, the enthusiasm remained undimmed.

The day of the workshop dawned with a sense of magic lingering in the air. As our small group gathered, there was an unspoken understanding that we were embarking on something special. With open hearts and eager minds, we shared our struggles and triumphs, creating a space where vulnerability was met with empathy, not judgment. One attendee, in an act of courage, brought along a lifeless plant–a tangible symbol of the challenges she faced on her journey. And in that moment, something beautiful happened. Instead of pity or ridicule, there was an outpouring of support and encouragement, a collective determination to nurture not just our plants, but each other.

As the day ended, there was a palpable sense of connection, a shared bond forged in soil and sunlight. As we parted ways, promises were made to reconvene, to continue this journey together. The feedback that followed was nothing short of extraordinary. What began as a simple workshop had blossomed into something far greater, a sanctuary where plant lovers could not only cultivate greenery but cultivate self-love and mental well-being.

In that humble farmhouse, surrounded by kindred spirits, I realized that we weren't just building a community of plants; we were cultivating a garden of the soul. And in that sacred space, growth was inevitable. Engaging with customers face-to-face proved enlightening, as I gleaned wisdom from their experiences and realized my own worthiness of success. Each exchange chipped away at my self-doubt, leaving behind a sense of empowerment and an insatiable appetite for growth. Through the trials and triumphs of entrepreneurship, I learned to embrace fear as a catalyst for resilience, trusting in my ability to adapt and thrive in the face of adversity. And as my business flourished, so did my belief in my limitless potential.

These stories have shaped who I am today, teaching me valuable lessons about coping, self-care, and healing. Through my journey with plants, I've learned how to nourish myself, and now I want to share that with you. I'll provide care tips and show you how to create your own plant collection. Additionally, I'd love to introduce you to journaling as a powerful tool to support your healing process and help you nourish yourself along the way.

"Like plants, our growth is incremental. Every day is a step towards blooming."

Nurturing Growth:
The Journey of Starting a Plant Collection

Starting a plant collection can be an exciting and rewarding journey, but it can also bring a bit of nervousness. Before diving in, it's essential to reflect on why you want to start a collection, and what you hope to achieve by bringing new plants into your life. Consider your available space, the time you can dedicate, and the budget you're willing to invest. Remember, a plant collection isn't just about the plants themselves; it's about creating a supportive environment that includes proper lighting, suitable pots, sturdy shelving, and the right nutrients. Whether you're caring for a single plant or managing a flourishing indoor garden, it's crucial to set aside regular time for daily, weekly, and monthly maintenance. As you learn about plant care, consistently monitoring and tracking changes will help you understand what's working well and what areas may need improvement in your routine.

Journaling Prompts for Self-Reflection:

1. What motivates you to start or expand your plant collection, and how does it reflect your current needs or desires in life?

_____
_____
_____
_____

2. How do you balance your time, space, and financial resources when taking on new responsibilities or hobbies?

_____
_____
_____

3. In what ways do you create supportive environments for your growth, similar to how you care for your plants?

_____
_____
_____
_____

4. How do you stay consistent in maintaining your commitments, and what strategies help you when motivation wanes?

_____
_____
_____
_____

5. Reflect on how you track your personal progress. How does monitoring and adjusting your actions influence your success?

_____
_____
_____
_____

"Love is the flower you have to let grow."
John Lennon

Cindy Hernandez

The Art of Care:
Navigating the Challenges of Calathea

The Calathea family consists of some of the most stunning yet demanding plants, requiring specific lighting and environmental conditions to thrive. Originating from the tropical rainforests of South America, Calatheas have a rich history as ornamental plants prized for their vibrant foliage. In their natural habitat, these plants grow beneath the dense canopy, adapting to low light and high humidity, which explains their particular needs in a home setting. Owning a Calathea is an investment of both time and money, as they often require specialized care and equipment to ensure their well-being. These plants are best suited for experienced plant enthusiasts who have already mastered basic plant care and are prepared to dedicate significant effort to maintaining their collection. It's not uncommon for even the most diligent care to fall short, leaving the plant struggling to thrive, which can be incredibly frustrating.

Journaling Prompts for Self-Reflection:

1. What aspects of your life require extra care and attention, similar to a Calathea plant, and how do you feel about the effort involved?

_____

_____

_____

_____

2. Reflect on a time when you put your best effort into something, yet the outcome wasn't as expected. How did you cope with that experience?

_____

_____

_____

_____

3. How do you handle situations where your investment of time and energy doesn't yield the results you hoped for?

_____

_____

_____

_____

4. In what areas of your life do you see yourself growing or thriving, and what factors contribute to that success?

_____

_____

_____

_____

5. Consider a time when you felt frustrated by a lack of progress. What did you learn about patience and perseverance from that experience?

_____

_____

_____

_____

"Your mind is a garden. Your thoughts are the seeds. You can grow flowers or you can grown weeds."
Anonymous

Resilient Beginnings:
My Journey with Succulents

Succulents were the first plants I ever cared for, and they truly symbolize my personal growth. These hardy plants are known for their ability to survive tough conditions, making them perfect for beginners. Succulents have a fascinating history: They evolved in arid environments, which is why they store water in their thick, fleshy leaves. This unique trait allows them to bounce back from neglect or overwatering. Originating from regions like Africa and the Americas, succulents have adapted to thrive with minimal water. However, they still need some attention—make sure their soil dries completely between waterings to avoid overwatering. Each leaf can even grow into a new plant, symbolizing new beginnings and the potential for growth, just like my own journey.

Journaling Prompts:

1. How have you shown resilience in my own life, similar to how succulents bounce back from neglect?

_____

_____

_____

_____

2. What aspects of your life need a "drying out" period, where you might benefit from taking a step back before moving forward?

_____

_____

_____

_____

3. In what ways can you nurture my own growth, much like caring for a succulent, to ensure I am thriving?

_____

_____

_____

_____

4. How can I learn from the idea of starting fresh, as a succulent leaf creates a new plant, and apply it to a current challenge or opportunity?

_____

_____

_____

_____

5. Reflect on a time when you felt overextended or neglected. How did you recover, and what did you learn from that experience?

_____

_____

_____

_____

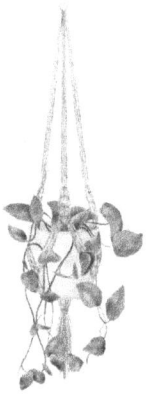

"Bloom where you are planted."
Mary Engelbreit

Cindy Hernandez

Nourishing Growth:
The Vital Role of Water in Plant Care

Watering is a crucial aspect of plant care, and understanding the different types of water and their uses can make a big difference in your plants' health. Each type of water—whether it's tap, distilled, rain, or alkaline—serves a unique purpose. For indoor plants, it's not just about how much water you give them, but also how often you check the soil's moisture. A good practice is to set aside one day each week to assess your plant's needs and water accordingly. Using clear pots can help you monitor root health and detect potential problems early. Remember, watering isn't just about pouring water from a bucket; it's about providing the right amount of nourishment to help your plant flourish.

Journaling Prompts:

1. How do you assess the "moisture" in my own life and decide what you need to thrive?

_____

_____

_____

_____

2. What are some ways you can better understand and respond to your own needs, much like choosing the right type of water for different plants?

_____

_____

_____

_____

3. Reflect on a time when a small change or adjustment made a big difference in your well-being. What did you learn from that experience?

_____
_____
_____
_____

4., How can you use the practice of regularly evaluating my needs to improve my personal growth and self-care routine?

_____
_____
_____
_____

5. In what areas of your life could you benefit from a clearer perspective, similar to how clear pots help monitor plant health?

_____
_____
_____
_____

"The creation of a thousand forests is in one acorn."
Ralph Waldo Emmerson

Cindy Hernandez

The Essential Foundation: Cultivating Growth Through the Right Soil

Soil is the foundation of healthy plant growth, much like a solid base is essential for building a strong structure. Just as we rely on a balanced diet to thrive, plants depend on the right soil to provide essential nutrients and support. The history of soil use in gardening dates back thousands of years, with ancient civilizations discovering the importance of different soil types for various plants. For instance, succulents need well-draining, gritty soil to prevent root rot, whereas plants like Begonias or Caladiums thrive in richer, bark-based soil. Choosing the right soil is crucial; it can make the difference between a flourishing plant and one that struggles to survive. Ensuring your plant has the proper soil type is not just a detail, it's a fundamental step towards successful gardening.

Journaling Prompts:

1. How do you ensure that you are creating a strong foundation for your personal growth and well-being?

_____
_____
_____
_____

2. In what areas of my life do you need to adjust, like choosing the right soil for different plants, to better support my goals?

_____
_____
_____
_____

3. Reflect on a time when the right "environment" helped you thrive. What elements were present, and how can you recreate that in other areas of your life?

_____

_____

_____

_____

4. How can you identify and address the needs in your life that are essential for your personal success, just as soil meets the needs of a plant?

_____

_____

_____

_____

5. What are some aspects of my life where you might be using the wrong "soil" or support system, and how can you make the necessary changes to improve?

_____

_____

_____

_____

"In a gentle way, you can shake the world."
Mahatma Gandhi

Cindy Hernandez

Illuminating Growth:
The Power of Light in Plant Care

The right lighting can transform your plant from a thriving beauty to a wilted mess. Lighting plays a crucial role in plant health, as it provides the energy plants need to grow and bloom. Historically, gardeners have long understood the importance of light, from ancient agricultural practices to modern indoor gardening. For example, some plants thrive in bright, indirect light, while others need direct sunlight to flourish. Placing a plant in an east-facing window is often ideal because it receives gentle morning sunlight, which is perfect for many indoor plants. This direction helps avoid the intense heat of afternoon sun, reducing the risk of sunburn. Transitioning from desert plants to indoor houseplants can be challenging, as I experienced myself. It took time and patience to learn the right lighting conditions for each plant. Once I figured out the best placements and when to use grow lights, it made a remarkable difference. Proper lighting is key to nurturing your plants and ensuring their vibrant growth.

Journaling Prompts:

I. How do you ensure that you are providing the right "lighting" or conditions for your personal growth and development?

_____
_____
_____
_____

2. Reflect on a time when finding the right environment or support system made a significant difference in your success. What elements contributed to this positive

change?

_____
_____
_____
_____

3. What areas of my life do you need to adjust to better meet my needs, similar to how plants need specific lighting to thrive?

_____
_____
_____
_____

4. How can you better understand and address the "light" needs of the people around you, ensuring they are supported and nurtured in the right way?

_____
_____
_____
_____

5. What are some practices or habits you could adopt to improve my personal and professional growth, just as grow lights enhance plant health?

_____
_____
_____
_____

*Like a cactus, I have a protective exterior
that shields me from negativity.*

Creating Balance:
The Importance of Ventilation
for Thriving Growth

Proper ventilation is crucial for healthy plant growth, making the difference between a thriving garden and a struggling one. Throughout history, gardeners have known that plants need the right environment to flourish. For instance, tropical plants require high humidity and good air circulation to stay healthy, while desert plants thrive in warm, dry conditions. A room that's too warm or too cold can disrupt this balance. Warm rooms can harm plants that need higher humidity, while cold rooms can cause desert plants to develop mold. Additionally, air conditioning can negatively impact your plant's health. If there's no airflow, the soil may dry out too quickly, causing wilting. Conversely, sitting plants directly in front of a vent can make them too dry and weak. Placing plants in an east-facing window is often ideal, as it provides gentle morning sunlight and good air circulation without the harshness of afternoon sun. Creating the right climate and ventilation for your plants ensures they receive the support they need to thrive.

Journaling Prompts:

1. How do you ensure that your environment is conducive to your personal growth and well-being?

_____
_____
_____
_____

2. Reflect on a time when adjusting your environment or

conditions made a positive difference in your life. What changes did you make?

_____

_____

_____

_____

3. In what areas of your life might you be creating conditions that hinder your progress, similar to how poor ventilation affects plants?

_____

_____

_____

_____

4. How can you better manage the balance between support and independence in your relationships and responsibilities?

_____

_____

_____

_____

5. What are some practices you can adopt to improve your personal "climate" or environment, ensuring you stay healthy and productive?

_____

_____

_____

_____

Write your own thoughts

_____

_____

_____

_____

_____

_____

_____

_____

_____

_____

_____

_____

_____

_____

_____

_____

_____

_____

_____

_____

_____

_____

_____

_____

Cindy Hernandez

Just as a houseplant purifies the air,
I bring positivity and clarity to those around me.

Cindy Hernandez

Nurturing Growth:
The Essential Tools for a
Thriving Plant Collection

Starting a plant collection involves more than just choosing the right plants; it also requires investing in the proper equipment and resources to keep them healthy and thriving. Understanding the needs of each plant will guide your decisions. Some plants are low-maintenance and only need basic care, such as light, water, soil, and air. However, other plants require additional tools like a humidifier to maintain the right moisture levels. Whether you have just one plant or a whole garden, you'll need essentials like fertilizers, neem oil, and other nutrients to support their growth. As you build your collection, you'll face choices about whether to buy ready-made plant care products or make your own solutions. Since 2020, plant care technology has advanced significantly, with many companies offering specialized products that simplify the process. Investing in the right equipment ensures your plants not only survive but thrive, making your gardening experience rewarding.

Journaling Prompts:

1. How do you determine the right "equipment" or resources needed to support your personal goals and projects?

_____
_____
_____
_____

2. Reflect on a time when investing in the right tools or resources made a significant difference in your success.

What was the outcome?

_____

_____

_____

_____

3. What are the essential "elements" you need to thrive in your personal and professional life, and how can you ensure you have them?

_____

_____

_____

_____

4. How can you balance the time and money you invest in your personal growth, similar to managing plant care tools and resources?

_____

_____

_____

_____

5. In what areas of my life could you benefit from upgrading or adjusting your approach to achieve better results?

_____

_____

_____

_____

Write your own thoughts

_____

_____

_____

_____

_____

_____

_____

_____

_____

_____

_____

_____

_____

_____

_____

_____

_____

_____

_____

_____

_____

_____

_____

_____

_____

_____

_____

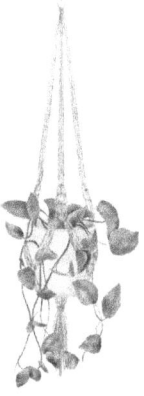

I am as resilient as a houseplant, capable of overcoming obstacles and growing stronger with each challenge. Plant the seed of desire in your mind and it forms a nucleus with power to attract to itself everything needed for its fulfillment.

Embracing the Cactus:
A Unique Connection

If I could identify with any plant in my collection, it would definitely be a cactus! This remarkable plant reflects both my physical and spiritual journey. Whenever I'm vending, and a cactus is present, it often sparks curiosity and a little fear. People frequently ask how I handle them without getting pricked by their sharp spines. Proper equipment is essential when caring for a cactus; gloves and tongs can help prevent those painful pokes. Despite taking precautions, I still occasionally get jabbed.

When I take a step back and observe how nature has designed the cactus to thrive in its ecosystem, I appreciate its beauty even more. The thorns serve as protection against hungry animals in the desert, while the large, fleshy stems store precious water. Cacti have a thick, waxy coating that reduces water loss, ensuring they survive in harsh environments. Their unique root systems are also adapted to absorb large amounts of water quickly after it rains, while their upper surfaces deflect the intense sunlight.

I love keeping cacti in my garden and using them to create stunning terrariums. There are countless fascinating features of these resilient plants, and I could talk endlessly about their beauty, which often goes unnoticed.

In the end, the cactus teaches us that even the toughest exteriors can hide remarkable resilience and beauty inside.

Journaling Prompts

1. How do you connect with the idea of resilience in your own life?

_____

_____

_____

_____

2. What are some "thorns" or challenges you face that help you grow?

_____

_____

_____

_____

3. How do you ensure you are nurturing your own needs, similar to how a cactus stores water?

_____

_____

_____

_____

4. In what ways do you protect yourself from external challenges, like the cactus protects itself?

_____

_____

_____

_____

5. Reflect on a time when you found beauty in something or someone that is often overlooked. What did you learn?

_____

_____

_____

_____

Write your own thoughts

_____

_____

_____

_____

_____

_____

_____

_____

_____

_____

_____

_____

_____

_____

_____

_____

_____

_____

_____

_____

_____

_____

_____

_____

_____

_____

_____

_____

A plant in nature endures both sunshine and rain and it doesn't know which helped it grow more. It is difficult to say if the hardships in life or the fun times did me the most good.

The Pothos:
A Resilient Gem in Any Collection

The pothos plant is often underrated, yet it deserves a special place in every plant collection. I remember when I first started my journey as a vendor. At one event, someone commented that my plants looked "basic." I was puzzled; how could such a beautiful and versatile plant be considered basic? In that moment, I realized that negativity can always exist, but my upbringing taught me to focus on the positives. The pothos is a fantastic choice for anyone, whether you're a beginner or an experienced plant lover because it comes in so many varieties. It's known for being adaptable and can thrive in a range of conditions, making it perfect for my workshops.

To take care of a pothos, all you need is some basic equipment like pots with drainage holes and well-draining soil. Regularly checking the moisture level and providing indirect sunlight helps the plant flourish. Pothos plants have a rich history, originally hailing from Southeast Asia, and they have been popular houseplants for many years due to their air-purifying qualities and ease of care.

In the end, the pothos teaches us that even the simplest plants can bring beauty and resilience into our lives.

Journaling Prompts

1. How do you handle negativity or criticism in your life?

_____

_____

_____

_____

2. What qualities do you see in yourself that are similar to the adaptability of the pothos?

_____

_____

_____

_____

3. Reflect on a time when you bounced back from a challenging situation. What helped you?

_____

_____

_____

_____

4. How do you nurture your own growth, just as you would care for a plant?

_____

_____

_____

_____

5. In what ways can you celebrate the simple yet beautiful aspects of your life?

_____

_____

_____

_____

Write your own thoughts

_____
_____
_____
_____
_____
_____
_____
_____
_____
_____
_____
_____
_____
_____
_____
_____
_____
_____
_____
_____
_____
_____
_____
_____
_____
_____
_____
_____

You made it through the grief, you can make it through the healing. Just like when a plant's leaves turn yellow and fall off.

Cindy Hernandez

The Monstera:
The Star of Any Plant Collection

When it comes to popular houseplants, the Monstera is like the guest everyone eagerly waits for to kick off the party. This plant boasts several species, making it a standout in any collection. From the well-loved Monstera deliciosa to the rare and pricey Monstera "Crème Brûlée, each variety adds a unique touch. Many people often wonder why these plants can be so expensive. The answer lies in several factors: the difficulty of propagation, the unpredictability of variegation, and their high demand. Collecting these plants is almost like collecting baseball cards, with some specimens fetching five-digit prices!

To properly care for a Monstera, it's important to use the right equipment, such as pots with good drainage and a well-aerated potting mix. These plants thrive in bright, indirect light and need regular watering, allowing the top inch of soil to dry out between waterings. Originally from the tropical rainforests of Central America, the Monstera not only enhances your space but also helps purify the air.

In the end, the Monstera is more than just a trendy plant; it's a captivating symbol of beauty and resilience that can brighten up any home.

Journaling Prompts

1. What qualities do you admire in the Monstera, and how do they reflect in your own life?

_____
_____
_____

_____

2. How do you handle the challenges of pursuing something you desire, like the rarity of a prized plant?

_____
_____
_____
_____

3. Reflect on a time when you felt "in demand" or appreciated. How did that make you feel?

_____
_____
_____
_____

4. What are some things you've collected in your life, and what do they mean to you?

_____
_____
_____
_____

5. In what ways do you nurture your own growth, just as you would care for a Monstera plant?

_____
_____
_____
_____

Write your own thoughts

Just like a plant that thrives when neglected you can carry yourself through your hardest days, when the people you counted on are nowhere to be found.

A Plant Collection to Inspire Curiosity: Everything is you

If you're looking for plants that will turn heads and spark conversations, the Begonia family is the perfect choice. These beautiful plants are some of my favorites, adding a touch of elegance to any collection. Alocasia, often called "Jurassic Park" plants, stand out with their unique shapes and striking leaves. Caladiums are another personal favorite. Their vibrant foliage brings joy, but they do go dormant in winter, creating a bittersweet emotional connection to their beauty.

Caring for these plants requires the right tools and techniques. Proper pots with good drainage and a well-balanced potting mix are essential for their growth. Most of these plants thrive in bright, indirect light, and they enjoy regular watering—just be careful not to overwater!

In addition to Begonias, Alocasia, and Caladiums, there are countless other varieties to explore, like Aloe Vera, Zamioculcas zamiifolia or "ZZ plants", and even carnivorous plants. Each brings its own charm and story to your garden. I hope you enjoyed discovering these plants as much as I have, and that they inspire you on your journey of gardening and healing.

Journaling Prompts

1. What draws you to the unique qualities of plants like Begonias and Alocasia?

_____
_____
_____

_____

2. How do you connect emotionally with things that go dormant or change, like the Caladium?

_____
_____
_____
_____

3. Reflect on a time when something unexpected sparked your curiosity. What did you learn?

_____
_____
_____
_____

4. What tools or resources do you use to support your personal growth and well-being?

_____
_____
_____
_____

5. How has your experience with gardening influenced your journey toward healing?

_____
_____
_____
_____

Write your own thoughts

_____
_____
_____
_____
_____
_____
_____
_____
_____
_____
_____
_____
_____
_____
_____
_____
_____
_____
_____
_____
_____
_____
_____
_____
_____
_____

Acknowledgement page

I would like to express my heartfelt gratitude to everyone who played a part in bringing this book to life.

This book would not be possible without the strength and resilience of my mother. She is the most supportive person I have ever met, and her example of a strong woman is invaluable.

To my spiritual Mother Lupita: Thank you for being the teacher I needed when I was at my lowest. You celebrated every single one of my highs with joy and I really appreciate you.

My sisters of the Luna Circle: You are truly remarkable and admireable women who have lifted me higher than I ever thought I could fly.

To my family: Thank you for your unwavering support and love. Your encouragement kept me going during the toughest times.

To my friends: I appreciate your patience and understanding as I poured my heart into this project. Your belief in me fueled my passion.

To: Sam, JP, Davina, and Gabby: Your guidance and insights were invaluable. Thank you for sharing your wisdom and encouraging me to explore my voice.

To my plants: You have taught me lessons of patience, resilience, and the beauty of growth.

To my readers: I hope this book resonates with you and brings comfort and inspiration.

About the author

Cindy Hernandez is a first generation Mexican/Salvadoran American and mobile plant shop owner. Born and raised in Los Angeles County, California. Cindy Hernandez has been a creative person since she was a child. In 2019, she found ways to combine her crafty skills and love of mental health and nature by caring for houseplants and cacti and creating workshops that are fun, empowering and healing to those who are struggling with depression, anxiety and other mental health concerns all over Los Angeles, Orange and San Bernardino counties in California. When she wants to relax, she enjoys her time traveling and dancing with her friends.She lives in Bellflower,California with her family and pets.

As we navigate the complexities of life, we may find comfort in the simple act of nurturing—whether it be plants, relationships, or our own well-being. I hope this book has inspired you to cultivate your own garden of resilience and reflection.